The Book of Love

The Book of Love

DAVID C SHELTON

Library of Congress Control Number		2021916320
ISBN:	Hardcover	978-1-6641-8952-2
	Softcover	978-1-6641-8951-5
	eBook	978-1-6641-8950-8

Print information available on the last page.

Rev. date: 08/10/2021

To order additional copies of this book, contact:
Xlibris
844-714-8691
www.Xlibris.com
Orders@Xlibris.com
831705

I want to dedicate this book to the adolescent me
and anyone who has ever failed to understand
just how important it is to love yourself.

The love that you deserve to have is
in your possession. It's time you give
it to the most important person in
your life, and that person is you.
You are beautiful, you are awesome,
and you are fabulous.

Love yourself.

It's your turn to shine now, so start shining.

CONTENTS

Words from the Author

Eight years ago, Bitcoin was at $500 a share. Today it's at $55,000 a share. It has risen and fallen throughout the years.

If you invested in Bitcoin eight years ago today, you're glad you stayed with it and did not throw in the towel when the stocks were low, right?

Eight years ago, I was homeless (lost all I had in a home fire.) Today I'm living my dreams, literally. I'm doing things I've only dreamed of.

My life has been through hell and back, but what if I gave up on believing in myself, investing in myself? I would've never been able to see just how high my stocks could go.

Now don't get it twisted. My stock is still going higher, although some people did withdraw their investment in me because they stopped believing in me and I might've let them down. However, I am thankful I decided to continue to believe in myself and stay the course.

Whatever you do, know that you must believe in *who you are*. Stay the course, finish the battle, and don't give up.

Please understand that your stock will rise and will fall, but stay the course.

People who are here today will be gone tomorrow, and that's okay. You make sure you don't give up. Your stock will rise; just hold on.

Why? Because "weeping may endure for a night, but joy comes in the morning" (Psalm 30:5).

The morning brings the sun to shine on you, and every time the sun rises and you see it, it's a message to let you know that *your life is not over*!

So get up and go hard today. Go after your dreams, invest in yourself, and be thankful for all you have and for all you have lost.

In the words of my favorite concert band Maze and Frankie Beverly: "I'm shining. Can't you see I'm shining?"

Now go and shine!

Chapter One

The Risk Is Steep

Your purpose is greater than what others want from you or what this world requires from you. Just be yourself.

Failure to fall in love with yourself will cost you in the end.

The risk you face when there is no self-love can send your life into a constant downward spiral. The penalty will be your sacrifice of happiness, peace, and healthy relationships.

After my first marriage, I realized that there was a lot of bad behavior in me. My relationships were not bad because "it all went wrong one day." It was always wrong.

I just happen to find out one day, and here is what I found out:

To have healthy relationships, it is necessary to have two healthy people.

To have a loving relationship, it is necessary to have two loving people.

The primary goal in a relationship is to fall in love. But you will have to find two people who have fallen in love with themselves first.

Love isn't love until it's given.

Please understand that you must give love to yourself before you can give it to someone else.

You need to know what it feels like to be loved by you before you allow someone to come in and force-feed you their idea of the love you want.

There are some people out there who need to seek help and find a good therapist ASAP.

I want you to understand that it is okay to start looking for help, which may be for you. It certainly worked for me.

On the other hand, there are those who just need to examine themselves thoroughly, and you may just happen to be that person.

Think about it

- to be able to right some wrongs,
- to move on from the anger that lives inside,
- to allow the child you used to be a chance at forgiveness,
- to learn how to forgive,
- to stop being super sensitive to everything,
- to be happy with who you are, and
- to be able to love yourself better than anyone else could.

Chapter Two

Who Did This to You?

Okay, everyone, let's keep it 100 percent. If you hate yourself or feel as if you don't deserve love, it's because something happened to you, something as simple as a phrase, a remark, a bully, a parent, a sibling, an abuser, or even a teacher.

Simply put. Hurt people hurt people. And somewhere down the line, a hurt person will hurt you.

We are human beings, and we all have feelings. Sometimes those feelings can be feelings of hurt.

The outcome from years and years of hurt will be determined depending on how you relieved yourself from the hurt.

Whether you were hurt as a child, as an adolescent, or as an adult, revealing or releasing is always important to living a healthy lifestyle, and you will be able to be loved and give it.

The pain of self-hatred can be due to different reasons. Abusive parenting or childhood trauma can prevent the development of self-esteem.

Perfectionism can lead people to believe that they will never be good enough, or having dissatisfaction with a particular trait, such as intelligence or appearance, can lead to doubt and inadequacy. A grave error, such as a betrayal or crime, can also fuel self-loathing.

Withholding the pain results in you releasing it onto others—your wife, your girlfriend, your husband, your coworkers, a social media post, your boyfriend, or your children.

You see, those closest to you will suffer your wrath. If you never seek help, it will eventually destroy your relationships.

Either way, this book is only the interpretation of self-therapy through my eyes.

This is not rocket science to me, but it is reality. So here is a good question to start with.

As children, we come into this world innocent. We enter this world with no fear, no malice, no emotional pain.

So how does a person go from an innocent child to a pain swollen adult?

How do you fix this?

It took me years, but I finally found out that I was the only one who could fix it.

Now to all my fellow Christians, it's not that I don't feel God can fix it, but even the Bible says,

> *If anyone says, "I love God" but hates his brother, he is a liar. For anyone who does not love his brother, whom he has seen, cannot love God, whom he has not seen.* (1 John 4:20 NIV)

The context in which I'm speaking has everything to do with loving God's creation, who happens to be you.

Self-love is a learned tactic. It is a belief system.

Self-hate is also learned, and you also must believe the false report to hate yourself.

Who taught you to hate you?

What happened to you to convince you that you were ugly, stupid, or not loved?

What made you believe those things?

We are fully aware that the hurt comes from a place. But what place?

Our purpose in life is just to become more of who we are. But if you are not okay with who you are, neither will anybody else be.

We spend so much of our lives trying to be accepted, to prove ourselves to other people, and to blend in that sometimes we stop prioritizing our true selves.

So the pain accrued from something someone said or did to you. That does not mean that you must believe it. You have a choice.

Believe *the truth* or believe *the lie.*

The truth is that you deserve to give yourself a chance at living without looking to be validated. *The truth is, it is none of your business how people feel or think about you.* The truth is that learning to love yourself is the greatest love of all.

Many of us still have that high school mentality that if we are loved by others, we will love ourselves, so we try to fit in or seek acceptance.

We only love ourselves when our actions match up with who we really are.

Start making a list of your qualities, likes, strengths, and passions. Then become more of that unapologetically.

Get rid of the activities or traits that do not feel true to you and fill up the empty space with more you-ness.

For example, find out what makes you feel alive, and then do it more often, or pick out your truest personality traits (quirky? compassionate? hilarious?) and bring them into work life, relationships, and the time you spend alone.

Every work goal, wellness intention, and daily schedule should support becoming more of who you really are.

Chapter Three

Forgiveness

Anger makes you smaller, while forgiveness forces you to grow beyond what you were."

—Chérie Carter-Scott

He who controls the past controls the future.
He who controls the present controls the past.

—George Orwell

Forgiveness is a challenge. It can take years or sometimes even a lifetime or longer to forgive. But many of us find it more difficult to forgive ourselves than to forgive others.

Unforgiveness creates anger, resentment, stress, sleep issues, and even physical problems.

In addition, someone who did these things to us may become so ingrained in our thoughts that we end up repeating that same offense ourselves.

Living life with the unforgiveness of ourselves is like living life believing that there is a looming anvil over our heads waiting to drop down at any moment, like Wile E. Coyote.

When we release ourselves and no longer feel like we are going to be punished spontaneously and brutally, we release that throbbing worry and live a life of freedom.

Forgiving You

If your car needs to be repaired, you wouldn't take it to the dentist, would you?

But that is exactly how some people approach relationships—broken down and looking for someone unqualified to fix them.

A husband, wife, boyfriend, and girlfriend are all not qualified to help fix you. Sex and drugs are not the answer. They cannot help you find the answer, because the only one who can fix you is *you.*

You must create your own healthy environment and allow yourself the opportunity to be healthy mentally and physically, as well as develop a healthy relationship. But to have a healthy relationship, you must be "love available," meaning you must be available to give and receive love. To some, that might seem simple.

Introducing the first contestant of forgiveness: you.

The unanimous disappointment of loving yourself is to hold on to things we have done in the past. It could have been an embarrassing moment that preyed on your mind to this day, or maybe it was a serious oversight, a flaw, or a major error that you are still letting define you.

If you cheated in a relationship, betrayed a friend, got fired from a job, or could recall every single humiliating moment since you were a kid, you might be holding on to evidences that you are not lovable.

(*Self-esteem* is a term used in psychology to reflect a person's overall emotional evaluation of his or her own worth. Low self-esteem is when you don't like yourself or you feel bad about yourself.)

Forgiving Others

Now introducing the second contestant to forgive: everybody else and everything else you have been holding on to.

Forgiveness allows you to bury the hatchet. This is the process of moving forward. It brings peace to the soul.

     Muster up compassion to those who have wronged us.

Why should you forgive? So that you can live a free and stressful life.

Imagine a world of no pain and no more hurt.

When you cannot forgive, you create a force field that surrounds you. This force field keeps you from being hurt. The force field helps you to protect yourself. But the force field only protects you. It causes you to put blame on others and to not see yourself.

Pointing fingers is usually the tactic used, specifically in a childlike manner—pushing all the blame off themselves and on to others, not being held responsible for their actions but holding others to theirs.

To be able to give and receive real love, you must own up to your flaws.

Through forgiveness, you can look at your mistakes, your flaws, and your misdirections, and this allows you to finally let go of others for their mistakes, flaws, and misdirections.

We are all human, which means that we all make mistakes. It's inevitable. It's been said that the only things that are certain in life are death and taxes, but I will add one more lifetime guarantee: screwing up.

We will all have to forgive ourselves at some point for making a mistake, doing something wrong, being human, and simply screwing up.

I believe in God. And I also believe that he is the creator of all.

We can't give what we don't have. In the same way, we are guaranteed to make mistakes, and those with whom we have relationships will make mistakes.

We can forgive others once we forgive ourselves, and that results in healing and peace.

The weak can never forgive. Forgiveness is an attribute of the strong. (Gandhi)

We don't always need to be strong, but we always need to be growing. Growth and development should never stop. And I think that's what Gandhi meant in this quote. By constantly growing, we can achieve our goals and create a life that we love.

A familiar passage of the scripture says,

> For God so loved the world that he gave his only begotten Son. (John 3:16 NIV)

Notice that the relationship that God had with his people was him giving love, meaning you do not really know love until you give a sacrifice worthy to receive the side-eye from onlookers.

Understand that this love is great, but you need to know that you have to love yourself this way first. If you do not, you will not be able to love others this way.

Love is giving, not taking.

It is free to give and free to receive. There is no pressure in love.

But there are love imitations that look like love, sound like love, but it is not loving.

Imitators come in all shapes and sizes. They will love you, but not love themselves.

Now I want to remind you that I have had my share of disastrous relationships. But I, too, had to learn how to make myself "love available" through the help of my Creator, prayer, friends, family, and spiritual guidance. I am a testimony of someone who has finally become "love available."

My first lesson was the lesson of forgiveness.

> Before you can forgive, you have to be forgiven.

I taught myself to be open and be honest with myself about what happened to me in my past. I embraced the one who was hurt first—*me*.

By embracing that hurt as a child or adolescent, you allow yourself room to move on.

Sometimes you must go back in your mind and see where you lost yourself, where you gained your anger, where you developed your hurt, where you first felt the void or the pain.

We must do a redevelopment process to help develop the person you are supposed to be.

I would like to let you into my own self-therapy session. It might not work for everyone, but it did work for me.

So relax and allow your mind to be transformed to the past. Close your eyes. Allow yourself to see yourself as a child or as an adolescent, or whenever the event(s) occurred that you feel caused you to lose who you are.

Can you see them yet?

After you can ask the younger you to come close, ask the younger you (whenever you were hurt) to even sit upon your lap. Look that younger you in their eyes and tell them, "It's going to be okay."

Have a conversation with that child/adolescent/adult. Let that child know that they did nothing wrong and should no longer be ashamed or afraid because they have been forgiven.

Watch the reaction of your inner self. Give the younger you a chance to respond, but continue to inform them that everything is now okay. Tell your inner child that they no longer must be angry, hurt, or sad.

Allow yourself time here and know that you have just freed yourself finally!

Now you are ready to forgive others so that you can move on. But wait . . .

What if this does not work? What if this does not work for you?

My answer is simple. Keep trying and keep trying. The Bible teaches us forgiveness.

> Then Peter came and said to Him, "Lord, how often shall my brother sin against me and I forgive him? Up to seven times?" And Jesus said, "I do not say to you seven times. But seventy times seven." (Matthew 18:21)

Simply put. Forgiveness is for you. You need it like you need to exercise. You need it like you need water to survive. You need it like you need energy food. Forgiveness is necessary for healthiness. If you do not have it, you cannot live.

So live and forgive and live some more. Smile, because today is a good day.

Chapter Four

The Scar

I was forever coming home. with a scratch or cut from schoolyard play. My mother would remove the band aid, clean the wound and say, "Things that are covered up don't heal well."

—Bishop T. D. Jakes

When I was four years old, I fell down a flight of steps inside my home. To the surprise of many, I did not cry, nor was I hurt.

But in the process of getting myself up off the floor, I put my hand on top of a drinking glass, which gave me leverage. But to my dismay, the glass gave way under my hand and broke into pieces.

I was cut from the inner of my thumb to the far side of my wrist. I remember the pain being so bad. It would be the first of many stitches in my life, but because of the scar, it would be the one remembered most.

To this day, I am reminded of the accident, not because I can still feel the pain but because I am only reminded of the scar that is left.

As a matter of fact, I really feel like it would have been just another forgotten moment if it had not been for the scar.

Honestly, every now and then, I look at my hand and remember. I can honestly say that I may never get rid of the scar, but I no longer feel the pain.

These emotional pains can live with you for a long time. So what if I told you that "if you let go of the emotions, you can also let go of the emotional pain that you carry"?

What if I told you that the reasons you are not happy is that *you* will not let go of the emotions?

If for that one moment you wanted happiness, would you give it a chance? Would you allow yourself the opportunity to have happiness? Do you want to be happy? (Please take the time to answer these questions.)

Women and men experience emotional pains that tend to have a huge effect on their life years later.

These emotional pains can be equivalent to physical traumas. These experiences could lead to dangerous actions or even cause you to live in dangerous situations.

Emotional pain could have you in places of using relationships as a crutch to survive. Those who fall into this will place the weight of the issues onto a partner or even a friend, which will produce the unhealthiest of relationships.

Not letting go of the emotional pain will cause you to pass this pain onto others. Once again, "Hurt people hurt people."

Too Much Junk in the Trunk!

I work out of my vehicle, and usually on a Sunday, I clean up my truck. This week, I had to clean it early. Had to use it to take my kids out because my SUV was down.

I went to clean up my truck, and to be honest, I was not aware how much junk I collected over a one-week period—water bottles, gum and candy wrappers, a McDonald's bag, a caramel frappe cup, a caramel mocha coffee cup, QT 32 oz cup, peanuts, sunflower seeds, paperwork from my job, and a lot more.

Now if I wanted my kids to ride with me, or anyone for that matter, how could they ride with no room in the vehicle?

How can anyone be this messy and expect for someone to be comfortable riding?

If I could collect that much in my car in one week physically without trashing anything, imagine mentally and spiritually what can be collected throughout a lifetime without letting go of the pain.

And then we expect others to come into our lives and ride. How dare you make someone else's life uncomfortable and heavy just because your life is that way?

You need to stop and start cleaning before you invite another person into your messy life.

And if you are not able to clean it, I know a good detail shop to refer you to. The name of the shop is Forgiveness and Release. If you start with that, your life will start looking brand-new.

The average person who seeks therapy for their personality traits is looking for happiness, looking to relieve the pain, and looking to move on.

You control your happiness and sad moments. You control the low self-esteem and your path in self-development.

The example of the scar is the same process of letting go of past hurts.

Because we are human, we are emotional. Therefore, if you allow your past hurts to come into your present, you will destroy your future.

Holding on to your past is causing you to be hindered today. You must let go so that you can experience freedom.

Sometimes the scar goes back to when you were children and have yet to move on. So if you live in the past, you deny yourself from living in the present.

Unfortunately, sometimes life is not fair. For example, in the game of cards, you are dealt a hand. Good or bad, you still must play the game.

Life deals us all a hand, some better than the other, but you only get one life to live.

But just because you're dealt a bad hand does not mean you must lose. You are only a loser when you give up. When you decide to give up fighting for yourself, then that's when you can take the *L*.

Do you want to?

But you will forever be a winner if you never stop fighting to get better.

You are not your emotions, and you are not married to them. You do not have to be devoted to the pain. You can let it go. You must see that it is the pain that is hurting you the most.

This is one of the primary reasons why relationships fail. You cannot be in a bad relationship with yourself and expect a good relationship with your mate.

Now for those of you who doubt what I'm saying, I understand. But you must keep trying.

'Tis a lesson you should heed: Try, try, try again. If at first you don't succeed, try, try, try again. (William Edward Hickson)

I don't care what you face; you cannot give up. Fight for yourself and your sanity.

If you are dealing with alcohol abuse, sex addiction, weight loss, drug addiction, and gambling addictions and if you fail, try again.

Do not give up on yourself. You are worth this fight. If you do not fight for yourself, who will?

Just like before, this may not work for everyone, but it worked for me.

Look at the situation or the situations that continue to bring forth the pain. Not only do you remember the situation but you also still carry the pain of the issue from when it took place.

Imagine that issue as something as simple as an orange. You squeeze and squeeze until juice runs out, but you continue to squeeze.

You squeeze harder, but nothing comes out anymore. But you continue to squeeze until your hands start to hurt.

So at this point, it is hurting you more to hold on to it. You almost do not realize that you can let it go, but you can.

Ask yourself a question here:

- Can I let this go? Yes or no?
- Can I let _____ (fill in the **name** here) go?
- Can I let _____ (fill in your **issue** here) go?

(Please take the time to answer these questions.)

Now please answer yourself.

It does not matter whether you answer yes or no. Just answer one of the two. Because when you do, you have just admitted that you are holding on to something that is hurting you.

These are just small steps to recovery.

You must see now that you have held on to the pain, and the pain is not holding on to you.

My friend, it's time to Open your hand and release the issue that pains you.

How did that feel?

Is it worth the effort to keep trying?

Then keep trying.

Repeat to yourself:

> I want to be free. I want to let go of my emotional pain so I can be free. I will allow myself the opportunity of the freedom I deserve.

My dear friend, please continue to release the pain and experience your freedom. You deserve this.

Chapter Five

Love the One You're With

If you're down and confused and you don't remember who you're talking to, concentration slips away, because your baby is so far away.

Well, there's a rose in a fisted glove. And the eagle flies with the dove. And if you cannot be with the one you love, honey, love the one you're with.

—Crosby, Stills, and Nash

Know Yourself

It's impossible to love yourself if you don't even know who you are.

What do you believe, value, and like?

Set Boundaries

We can become people-pleasers and be focused on meeting other people's expectations rather than being ourselves. And if you're enmeshed, you may not recognize that you have the right to make your own choices or set boundaries. Learn to say *no*!

Stop Comparing Yourself to Others

My older brother was a ladies' man and a smooth talker.

The neighborhood loved him, and every time someone compared us, I was reminded that I was deficient in these areas.

Comparing us, I didn't recognize my strengths; it only highlighted the areas I felt lacking in.

We compare ourselves to others, looking to see how we measure up.

The problem is that comparison only works to validate our fears and self-doubts. It never leaves us feeling better about ourselves.

We can always find someone who is thinner, drives a nicer car, or has a picture-perfect marriage and use them as proof that we're not as good or worthwhile as other people.

We compare ourselves to others because we feel unsure of ourselves. In conclusion, we end up feeling inferior.

Connect with Yourself

At times, we don't know what we feel or what we need because we're constantly numbing ourselves with *food*, *alcohol*, *drugs*, *electronics*, and *pornography*.

These are the quick fixes we use to make ourselves feel better.

Slow down, tune in, and listen to our bodies, thoughts, and feelings. Learn breathing exercises, yoga, or meditations. You must become mindful of *who you are*.

Trust Yourself

When you don't trust yourself, you're unsure what to think, feel, and believe. This can be very upsetting and confusing. A lack of self-trust makes almost everything in your life harder. However, your self-trust can be rebuilt.

As a man thinketh, so is he.

When I was a kid, I allowed myself to be hurt, believing I was not good enough, I was not thin enough, and I was not handsome enough.

Yes, I was teased by kids in school, heard chants of "Fat boy" or "Ugly." But *it was not* the ridicule of my peers that created the way I felt about myself. It was the way I thought about myself and the way I allowed myself to think about myself.

The way you think can speak volumes for your life.

If you tell yourself something, it becomes true. If you tell yourself "I am ugly," then trust me, you are now ugly. If you tell yourself "I am dumb," then trust me, at this point, you are now considered a big dummy.

One day I stopped. I stopped with the toxic talk. I stopped believing the lies. I began to look in the mirror, and I found out that I was a handsome black man. I fell in love with the skin I am in. I am sexy, I am fine, and I am smooth. I am a big teddy bear.

I began to speak into more of my life. I am rich. I am intelligent. I am an author, songwriter, singer, minister, encourager, father, friend, lover, and a hardworking man.

You speak life into your life. You speak life into your day. You speak life into your relationships. Whatever you say, whatever you speak, whatever you put into the air is what life has in store for you.

So watch what you speak. Watch what you declare.

We could start quoting songs back and forth. When it comes down to this subject, there are a lot of songs dedicated to love. But with all the songs that talk about love, just a few talks about loving yourself.

I think Crosby, Stills, and Nash hit the nail on the head. "The rose in the fisted glove" is an analogy of hiding the beauty you possess. "The eagle flies with the dove" is a way of saying that you chose to feel less than what you are, so then "if you can't be with the one you love, you should love the one you're with."

Self-love is a start to a healthy lifestyle. Because if you do not love yourself, how do you expect to love someone else?

You see, that moment when you find a good woman or a good man seems great at first, but if they lack self-love, the story will unfold sooner than later.

The one you need to love has always been there, and that one is *you*.

With all your looking for the right person to give you love, you look over the one most important person to love, and that is *you*.

So you attempt to find love "out there," but the love you are looking for is right there with you.

Therapy

Find the nearest mirror. Sit or stand; it does not matter.

Look at yourself. Look at your flaws, your features, and your problems/issues.

Now repeat after me.

Hi, my name is _____
(your name here).

God made me perfect. I am special. I
am beautiful. I am God's perfect creation.
I am good at _____ (fill
in the blank).

I enjoy _____ (fill in
the blank).

I am most helpful when I'm
_____ (fill in the blank).

People say I'm _____
(fill in the blank).

If there was one thing I could
do for the rest of my life, I would
_____ (fill in the blank).

You have just had your first courting session with
yourself. Continue to get to know you. You will find
out that you have a lot in common with yourself and
that there is a good man and a good woman "out
there" after all.

It is you. You are that person that you have been looking for.

> Well, there's a rose in a fisted glove.
> The eagle flies with the dove. And if you
> can't be with the one you love, honey,
> love the one you're with.

So why don't you nurture that relationship like you do with your best friend, mom, or significant other?

Loving yourself might be as simple as loving yourself in your very own love language.

Create a list of how you treat the people you love:

Do you text them to check in?

Do you surprise them, give them compliments, or wish them "Good night" before you go to bed?

However you treat the people you love should be the way you treat yourself too.

Check up on yourself, give yourself compliments, treat yourself regularly, or look in the mirror and say "Good night" before bed. As silly as it may feel at first, we all give love a certain way, and self-love is not any different.

Chapter Six

Change Your Environment

There's a reason why a tree's leaves change color in fall—it's a visual signal that it's adapting to its surroundings, prepping for what's ahead.

It could be equivalent to the morning sun rising and setting in the evening as a message to humanity that life isn't over.

Your environment, which includes your friends, colleagues, location, habits, and lifestyle, impacts you far more—for better or for worse—than you realize.

You can't make a significant, lasting change without altering some elements of your environment.

Ask yourself these two questions to better assess if your environment is helping you grow or holding you back:

The greatest commodity processed on earth is time. Time is the currency of the life. Currency is what you use to buy things (spending time wasting time.)

Everyone has the same amount of time, twenty-four hours, every day. Whatever you use your time for is what you become today.

But did you know you can control time?

You cannot stop time, go back in time, or travel to the future, but you can control it.

The answer is simply by planning. Planning will tell time how you are going to spend it. So without a plan, time is wasted. Focus heavily on planning.

For I know the plans I have for you," declares the LORD, "plans to prosper you and not to harm you, plans to give you hope and a future. Then you will call on me and come and pray to me, and I will listen to you. You will seek me and find me when you seek me with all your heart. I will be found by you," declares the LORD, "and will bring you back from captivity. I will gather you from all the nations and places where I have banished you," declares the LORD, "and will bring you back to the place from which I carried you into exile." (Jeremiah 29:11–14 NIV)

If you don't have a plan for your life, the wind of change is going to battle you left and right.

A storm is coming. There are storms ahead and soon to come—tornado season, hurricane season, etc.

A season is not permanent. A storm is a temporary convergence of natural currents and the elements reacting to and affecting the environment, impacting the normal cause of life.

Storms are natural. They come and go. A storm is a natural element (things that occur often). Rain, wind, water, and heat are elements we use and need, but when they converge in a unique way, they can kill us all.

The loss of a job, the death of a loved one.

Blessings come in seasons. Realize that it is what it is, just a season.

The greatest blessing in life is that life is seasonal. Whatever you go through, it will not last.

Decisions that come in seasons must consider the change that is coming. Do not make permanent decisions in seasonal distress. Don't throw your coats away just because it's ninety degrees in the summer.

We are running out of time. Reposition yourself. Change the way you think and function and the way you feel.

Your attitude changes everything. Your attitude changes people. Your attitude changes situations. Your attitude changes the outcome. Your attitude changes your finances. Your attitude changes your friendships. Your attitude changes your romance.

A change in your attitude can change you.

You create your atmosphere.

Chapter Seven

Stop Believing the Lies

Stop, look, and listen. If you have read this book this far, that means one or two things:

One, you are a true fan and would read anything I write.

Two, you have found yourself in these pages.

If you are a true fan, thank you. But if you have found yourself in these pages, it is time to stop and allow yourself a chance at being whole.

You need to hold yourself responsible for your actions. As a saying goes, *"Fool me once, shame on you. Fool me twice, shame on me"* (Chinese proverb).

Meaning that if you allow something to happen once and it is not what you expected, then get up, brush yourself off, and learn from it.

You cannot continue to do the same thing and get different results. If you return to the same results, that only means you are still following the same patterns. It might not look the same, but it is the same. If you want to have different results, try changing your approach to the whole outlook you have on relationships.

If you are someone who has been in a reckless relationship and now your new mate is great and does not remind you of the person you were in that reckless relationship, that's great!

You have learned from the pattern that you followed. You have changed your approach. But if you continue to find yourself in relationships that fail, you must change first before you can expect your relationships to.

See, even though you get what you want, it still does not make you better. You must learn how to seek happiness from within, not in someone or something.

Setting boundaries will let other people know that you expect respect, but more importantly, they let you know that you deserve respect.

Saying no when you mean no means you are putting your needs above others.

Maybe it is the coworker who asks for help when you are already swamped, the neighbor who needs a favor when you are exhausted, or getting guilted into a holiday event you do not feel comfortable attending.

Understand that every time you say yes when you want to say no, but other's opinions and needs above your own, which builds more evidence that you are not the priority.

A genuine yes or a yes that is in line with your best interest will make you excited without doubt or worry. Say yes when you mean yes and no when you mean no.

My dad used to say to me, "If it can make you happy, it can make you sad." Whatever can make you smile can make you frown. So if a person, place, or thing can make you happy, that same person, place, or thing can make you sad.

So in this case, it shows that you are not in control of your feelings and that others are. You allowing others to control how you feel proves that you are not ready to be in love. Not only that, but you are not ready to love someone.

That control is necessary—the control of your feelings, the management of your happiness and your sadness. You must be a master of yourself. You cannot allow others to master you. You must master yourself.

This book is designed to get you to be "love available." So stop, look, and listen to your heart.

Your heart is crying out to you, and the fact that you continue to overlook the cries within will only hurt you in the end.

Tell yourself the truth. Stop pretending that there is nothing wrong when plainly there is.

Finding yourself in an abusive (physical, verbal, and mental) relationship is an example of people not paying attention to their hearts first.

People not being honest with themselves will continue to lie to themselves, even giving themselves an excuse.

That woman did. That man did. But what is your part in it?

There is no doubt that everybody wants a fairy-tale relationship.

But in a fairy tale, there must be a transition of the two in the relationship, then they will live happily ever after.

But some would rather just live happily ever after and yet not have to face the transition to get there.

It is plain to see how you are not in control of your life. You have not started to forgive yourself. You have not fallen in love with me. You have not let go of the emotional pain. You have not given yourself a chance.

How then do you expect to fall in love when you do not know what love is?

How do you expect to give love when you do not know what love is?

How do you expect to be loved when you do not know what love is?

Until you do the first work, you cannot be available to love friends, family, kids, husbands, wives, girlfriends, and boyfriends.

To be able to have healthy relationships even with these people, you must be available.

Stop and ask yourself now, Does my past affect my present? Have all my relationships failed because of my mates? What has my role been in my relationships? Do I have complete control of my feelings?

(Please take the time to answer these questions.)

Create a mindset of excellence and a spirit of achievement! How you do anything is how you do everything. Make it your business to ensure that how you show up, what you say, and what you do reflect the best of who you are. You are to better your best.

Teach your mind to think and work like there is no tomorrow. You can change everything by changing one thing—your mind! You got it like that! Make it happen. You deserve it!

Are you aware that you were the cause of a lot of your heartache but you constantly point the finger?

Do you ever feel like the reason you do not have stable relationships is because of you? Or would you instead find someone else to blame?

Understand that sometimes you must see that you have the right to choose. And it is your choices that you must live with.

It is time you start making better choices and be honest with yourself. It is time to stare at the one in the mirror and start to own your actions. Waiting on your issue to resolve itself will not work. Just make a go at it.

Well, here is one main issue. Jesse and Sara should have never been married in the first place. How is it that we allow such things to happen?

As a good friend, an outspoken relative, or even a church minister, we have the right to point out the flaws that can cause division in a relationship. But the typical response is, "I told them to wait." Yes, but did you tell them why?

The truth is deserved. Sara and Jesse earned an opportunity to know about themselves before the marriage. Instead, they get into a relationship bound for disaster.

Like an airplane without wings, it would never fly. With truth, you will find a love that will lift you to the sky . . . (David C. Shelton)

Chapter Eight

Give Yourself a Chance

I am not happy because of some extraneous circumstance. I am happy because I choose to be.

—Morris E. Wray

When people get a sense of purpose in their lives, the value of time gets higher.

There are good and bad voices in all of us. Believe that they will not go away.

The bad voice will tear you down, make you feel as if you are incomplete because you were not raised with riches or a silver spoon in your mouth. The bad voice will constantly remind you that you cannot do something or that your dreams of being an entrepreneur, going to college, succeeding in life will never happen. The bad voice in your head will try to run distractions so that you will not focus on what is ahead. Distractions like lying in bed instead of getting up. Distractions like watching TV instead of setting your agenda. Distractions like getting involved with reckless activity instead of pursuing your goals for the day.

Soul-searching is healthy for you. You can take time to investigate yourself and see why you lash out on your mate, why you shut yourself down from your mate, or the fact that you turn to violence.

The Selfishness You Carry

Your search for love is not lost at all. Even if your relationship has gone bad, you can still be strong.

You can stand the test of time if you follow the steps given. You can find love, and you will be able to give love. You will be "love available."

People think that once they lose weight, get a great job, or find a solid relationship, then they will be healthy or feel happy.

But self-love is not conditional; it is a skill you achieve with practice.

And how do you practice?

You keep promises to yourself.

Confidence just means that you trust your own word: when you say you are going to do something, you do it. That means cooking dinner instead of getting takeout, waking up for that morning workout, and not going back to your ex (actually, we have all been there).

Keep in mind that following through with what you plan on doing is worth more than just achieving what you want. Building confidence and self-trust translates into self-love.

Participate in a play appraisal right now. When was the last time you did anything just for fun? How do you spend your free time alone that is not binge-watching Netflix?

If it is difficult (or impossible) for you to think of an answer, your incredibly stressful adult life has likely taken seniority over an especially important aspect of life: having fun.

The lack of self-love or constant self-judgment might be just because you are taking life too seriously.

Embrace regular "playtime" in your life by turning on music and dancing, doing something creative like coloring, or going to your local jungle gym and going on the monkey bars (bonus points as it doubles as a workout!). If you feel silly "playing," that is even more reason to.

No matter what your current relationship with food is like, the food you eat should be an act of self-love. Are you familiar with that old-school saying that you are what you eat? It is kind of true: food serves as information that tells our bodies what to do.

It is not about "good foods" you're supposed to eat versus "bad foods" you are not supposed to eat; it is about loving your body enough to nourish it with whatever makes it feel its best. After all, good health is the best gift you could ever give to yourself. Pleasure is a nutrient too, so also treat yourself to the foods you love without guilt, shame, or deprivation.

Here are the steps to follow:

- Forgive.
- Let go of the emotional pain.
- Love yourself.
- Move on.
- Be honest with yourself.

- Give yourself a chance to love again.

No one said it would be easy, but you can do it. Through the right channels, you can be successful.

I can't.

I don't think it's in me.

I want to do it but . . .

These are the excuses we continue to give when we see ourselves and respond to constructive information to help us do better.

Excuses are the coverings of flaws. And as living human beings, we all have flaws.

No more excuses. It's time to move on. It's like a second birth.

A familiar scripture in the Bible states that Nicodemus asked Jesus how he could have eternal life. Jesus told him to be born again.

That second birth is what I am speaking of. It makes you feel alive when you know why you are here.

As I sat and evaluated my life, I knew that someone else was to hear my story. I knew that I was qualified to help somebody who faced the things that I faced.

Maybe you do not know a protein from fat and care more about advantages or taste than nutrients, or maybe you have some basic food rules, like it stresses you out if you eat a slice of pizza or a piece of cake.

Your body feels bad after eating junk food. There is such a thing as junk food for the brain, and it makes your mind (and body) feel bad after consuming it.

The shows you binge, the podcasts you listen to, and the books you read feed you just as much as leafy greens and chickpeas.

Make sure you choose the most nourishing options:
Turn off the news.
Take a break from social media.
Stop watching TV that feels like a waste of time.
Read books that inspire you.
Listen to books that motivate you.

By the way, this also goes for your TikTok, Twitter, and Instagram feed:

Unfollow or mute anyone who does not make you feel inspired, encouraged, or happy.

Be more conscious and choosier with every way you are nourishing your body.

The Bible says, "They shall overcome by the word of their testimony and by the blood of the lamb."

If you have been in a failed relationship or you are currently in a failing relationship, before things get any worse, before you get into another relationship, seek help. Seek happiness. Do not continue to add to the pain.

Seek God. Whether you serve Jesus, Muhammad, or Buddha, it does not matter. Just seek help. Whether from friends, family, or a counselor, get help.

I am a living example that love is a beautiful thing. And being in a relationship is just as wonderful.

And if it had not been for my divine intervention, I would have never been in a place to have an option of giving love and receiving it healthily.

Today I am love available.

My sign is out hanging and posted. It has nothing to do with what someone can give me or show me. But it has everything to do with who I am and what I have become. I realized that everyone who wants a serious relationship is not ready for a serious relationship. But if you are looking to be in a serious relationship, make sure you are *"love available."*

Chapter Nine

Be Thankful

This just in:

Stop complaining about what you don't have and learn to be thankful for what you have.

You see, as a father, I know what it feels like to be appreciated and unappreciated. Many times in our lives, we hear our children say "Man, I wish I had this" or "I wish I had that." As a parent, you ask, "Well, what about the last one I bought you?"

You see, when you can appreciate what is already in your possession, it is not hard to get something new.

Stop complaining about the job that you have. Stop complaining about your woman or your man. Stop complaining about your home or your car. Start being thankful for what you have and watch and see that you will get the one that you want.

Learn how to be thankful, learn how to be grateful, and learn how to be glad.

Start now. Close your eyes for one minute and be silent. Now open your eyes and look around you and start to say these words:

Thank you for _____
(you fill in the blank).

Keep a gratitude journal and add to it every day.

Tell someone you love them and how much you appreciate them.

Notice the beauty in nature each day.

Nurture the friendships you have; good friends don't come along every day.

Smile more often.

Watch inspiring videos that will remind you of the good in the world.

Include an act of kindness in your life each day.

Avoid negative media and movies with destructive content.

Call your mom or dad more often.

Cook meals with love; think of the people you will feed.

Volunteer for organizations that help others.

Don't gossip or speak badly about anyone.

Spend quality time with your kids or your lover.

Remember to compliment your friends and family when they look good.

Write a card to someone you haven't seen in a while and tell them something nice.

Add to your gratitude list daily at least one more thing.

When you think of a negative thought, try to see the positive side of the situation.

Commit to one day a week when you won't complain about anything.

Try to note when people do a good job and recognize them when it's due at work.

Reward effort; if someone does something nice for you, do something nice for them.

Meditate with your gratitude list, giving thanks for all your good fortune.

Live mindfully, not worrying about the past or future.

Thank the people who serve you in the community—the shopkeeper, the bus drivers, etc.

Say thank you for the little things your loved ones do for you, things you usually take for granted.

Post quotes and images that remind you to be grateful around your house.

Call an elderly neighbor and say thank you for their presence in your life.

Call your grandparents and tell them you love them.

Embrace challenges and turn them into opportunities to grow.

Send love to your enemies or people you dislike.

Be thankful when you learn something new.

See the growth opportunity in your mistakes.

Help your friends see the positive side of life.

When times are bad, focus on your friends who are at your side. When times are good, notice and help others.

Make a gratitude collage; cut out pictures of all the things that you are grateful for.

Make gratitude a part of family life, and share it during mealtime. Practice gratitude at the same time every day to make it a habit.

Focus on your strengths.

Share the benefits of gratitude with family and friends.

Share gratitude each day by posting a tweet, Facebook post, or Pinterest.

Learn how to be thankful for everything that is around you right now and watch and see that your day will be a blessed day.

40 Things You Can Do to Fall in Love with Yourself

1. Realize that it is okay to make mistakes. Just make sure to learn from them, forgive yourself, and move on.
2. Make your health and wellness a top priority and always take care of yourself so you are ready to take care of others.
3. Follow your own path, not one that others want you to follow.
4. Find the humor in life and laugh like there is no tomorrow.
5. Relax and move with the flow of life by being unafraid of change.
6. Be adventurous by trying new things and taking more risks.
7. Have more intellectual curiosity and embrace creativity.
8. Try to find happiness with as many different people as you can.
9. Think for yourself instead of letting other people's opinions influence you too much.
10. Try not to judge people before you get to know them.

11. Be thankful for what you have now instead of thinking about what you do not have.
12. Wish well upon everyone equally and try to admire without envy.
13. Share your happiness with others instead of hoarding it all for yourself.
14. Do not try to change someone; love who they are now.
15. Enjoy the journey, not just the destination.
16. Know that happiness is bigger than any bank account.
17. Control negative thoughts so that they do not contribute to the outcome of your life.
18. Use your energy wisely because spending energy complaining, worrying, or being impatient is just wasted energy.
19. Be bold. Find the courage to change things that should be changed and accept that there are some things that cannot be changed.
20. Love your work. If you do not currently love what you do, figure out what you would love and take the first step toward that life.
21. Turn your discontent into a mystery and enjoy trying to solve it.
22. Face problems from different angles to find solutions.

23. Gain independence by realizing that on this earth, we are all dependent upon one another.
24. Change your perspective by taking on a wider view of things.
25. Do not waste time trying to bring disagreeable people around to like you.
26. Become the person you would like to spend the rest of your life with.
27. Be honest with yourself and others by saying what you mean and meaning what you say.
28. Treat people with respect and compassion.
29. Live in the now by loving the present and being aware of your thoughts and actions. Think happy thoughts and speak powerful words.
30. Try not to put things off until later.
31. Never hold grudges.
32. Face your fears head-on and try to do the things that you think you cannot do.
33. Spend time with people who make you happy while also not depending on other people for your own happiness.
34. Stand up for yourself and others and do not let anyone or anything hold you back.
35. Be yourself and love who you are now.
36. Be a participant in life rather than an observer.

37. Do the things that you love to do as much as you can.
38. Write out a list of goals and achieve them by doing them step by step. Do not give up when things get difficult.
39. Do something every day that makes you feel proud of yourself; commit to random acts of kindness whenever you get the chance.
40. And always keep on moving forward.

Lightning Source UK Ltd.
Milton Keynes UK
UKHW010221240821
389362UK00008B/492/J